THE KEY CONNECTOR

HOW TO BUILD AN EMPIRE
HELPING PEOPLE

By: Deloris Williams

The Key Connector

How To Build an Empire Helping People

by Deloris Williams

Trient Press

3375 S Rainbow Blvd

#81710, SMB 13135

Las Vegas,NV 89180

Ordering Information:

Quantity sales. Special discounts are available on quantity purchases by corporations, associations, and others. For details, contact the publisher at the address above.

Orders by U.S. trade bookstores and wholesalers. Please contact Trient Press: Tel: (775) 996-3844; or visit www.trientpress.com.

Printed in the United States of America

Publisher's Cataloging-in-Publication data

Williams, Deloris

A title of a book : The Key Connector

ISBN

Paperback : 978-1-953975-87-4

E-book : 978-1-953975-89-8

Table of Contents

Introduction

Whether you know me as the founder of Divine Connections magazine, have run into me at an event, or have been interviewed by me, you can see my values at first glance, the chief among which is my desire to help people. My problem with self-help is that the emphasis on "self" is present in such literature to a fault. When I look at my success, I realize that almost all of it comes from my focus on helping others. This book is yet another attempt to help others. And the idea is to sell you on the values that have helped me build my empire. Welcome to "How to Build an Empire Helping People."

You're Always In Demand

People often have a hard time selling not because they're not in demand but because they insist on selling what they want to push, not what others want to receive from them. If we remove sales and money from the equation, I guarantee that none of us have a problem with not being in demand. If anything, most of us are frustrated with the fact that we get asked for help or support too often. However, we do not consider it as a potential route to monetization because we're engaged in a pre-engineered journey.

For example, when someone asks you to watch their kids while they go to another city, you may not see how this could be a foundation for a new daycare business because you're too committed to finding a job as an engineer. You might have an engineering degree, but instead of opening doors for you, your refusal to look past it is actively shutting doors on you. The world will always put you in boxes, but it is your job not to seal yourself in one.

I have to wear different hats: I'm an editor, an interviewer, often a subscription seller, and of course, a writer. But I allow none of these hats to cover my eyes. Confirmation bias is the human tendency to only look for evidence that fits one's preconceived notions. This occurs in our day-to-day lives when we believe X or Y is our way to make money. We ignore A, B, and C in the process. If this book does anything, it opens your eyes up to every last possibility. More importantly, it reduces the effort required as it helps you build success from opportunities that come to you.

Help is always required. No one says, "nobody asks me for help," in a defeated tone. That's because our friends, neighbors, and even strangers ask us for help, usually in the form of service. If you pay attention, you'll realize that you get a certain type of help requested over and over. Across a long enough period, you can either build excellent efficiency with regards to this type of request or create a scalable resource.

If you have a small store in your neighborhood and tourists keep knocking on your door to ask you when the nearby shop opens, you can simply write "shop opens 9 am, I am not the owner" and stick it on your door. This is automation. If you get asked to help babysit kids, and you become exponentially better at it, that's efficiency. Now, let's talk about the help requested from me.

Responding With Excellence

Imagine showing up to your job and doing your worst. When you get called in by the manager, it definitely isn't about a raise. Would you be able to get a raise, though, by saying, "I will only do well if you give me more money"? That attitude doesn't fly in any transnational situation. And that's why people miss out on every opportunity in their lives. When help is requested, we don't act as if we're paid, and that's why we don't get paid. It's a vicious cycle of sorts.

My friends used to ask me for help, and I did just one thing differently than most people; I responded with excellence. This started back in high school, where I was socially competent. When people needed help with anything, they would ask if I had the information or a connection. I thought if some people need my help with a specific thing, many more may just not have the proximity or courage to ask for help. This is the crucial step in empire-building to pay attention: I not only helped everyone to the best of my ability but went and looked for others who might need support.

That's how my magazine was born. It started as a compilation of these resources. A one-stop-destination for the help people needed from me. It isn't enough to charge your friend to babysit her kids; you must understand that there are others who need their kids supervised but may not know you're in that business. That said, my personal example is different because I didn't seek to immediately monetize my service.

This brings me to the crucial question regarding monetization: should I charge? I say it isn't the matter of whether you should or you shouldn't (you should, of course), but it is a question of when you must start charging. This can vary from market to market. An online knowledge provider can lecture 10,000 people before deciding to create a paid course. We can't expect that level of free labor, in quantitative terms, from someone who repairs cars.

Simply going by the economics of supply and demand while factoring in average conversion rates, I would recommend that you keep your service/help free (and as excellent as if you were being paid) until you reach ten times the number of people you actually need to make money. In other words, if you need 100 customers to make a sustainable income, you should help a thousand people for free before you start monetizing your business.

Action Welcomes Exposure

Just like people insist on getting paid before helping, they insist on having an audience before creating anything worthy of an audience. Needless to say, this doesn't fare well for them in the short or the long run. I discovered early on that the more people I helped, the more exposure my platform got. That's where I decided to do it quarterly. With only four issues a year, it wasn't as time-consuming as it would need to be for me to start insisting on receiving money.

The question you must ask yourself is, "how much of this can I do without charging." We live on an economic planet, and there's a lot of money circulating. People are apprehensive about spending without witnessing excellence, but when they spend, they spend freely. Free work is better than paid advertising. Remember, people spend money to advertise only when they need a large enough volume that they cannot afford to serve for free.

For example, if you have a lemonade stall, you can afford to give everyone a drink for free the first day. But Coca Cola cannot serve its entire customer base a free drink. That's why they spend billions of dollars on ads: because spending billions on ads is cheaper than giving free coca-cola for a day. Coke spends 4 billion dollars of ads in a year while selling 1.9 billion units a day. It is literally cheaper to advertise.

But if you were to spend a hundred dollars on advertising your Lemonade stall instead of spending thirty on lemons and giving free lemonade, you'd be making the wrong choice. People trust the excellence they experience. Don't try to follow corporations' footsteps; they cannot afford to help people for free, you can. But your support must be within reason. Finding that frequency where you can afford to work for free is crucial.

I helped my peers with a quarterly resource because I could do so without demanding a full-time living wage. Now had I been putting out an issue every month, it would be impractical for me to do so without charging significant money. And the moment I started charging the same as industry magazines, I would have killed my exposure. You must recognize that you have to be willing to do free work until you have enough trust in the market. And you should do so with tact and within limits, so you don't starve yourself in the short-term with your eye on the long-term.

Move Fast and Slow

As I write this book, I have a part-time job and a part-time business. That's because transitioning from day job to business owner requires you to have a source of steady income, so you're not feeding yourself off your business but are feeding your business. People often look at businesses as a golden goose, while the more accurate way to look at it is like a child.

If you're on a ranch, you can't expect your newborn to help out the next morning. But if you feed that baby well, you're right he'll give you a helping hand. It's the same with a business; your business should first be fed before you can expect it to feed you. Too many people are too quick to try to serve themselves with their business. This is not the right call by a long stretch.

To make matters worse, they do it in the wrong order. They're slow as a tortoise when it comes to starting something, but when they do launch their "dream" venture, they're hasty as a hare in terms of making their thing the next Facebook or Tesla. That's not how you treat the things you love. Imagine adopting an eight-week-old puppy and insisting he learn to sit in a day, or you'll abandon it. If a person said that, would you believe he loves his dog? Then how can I believe you love your dreams if you insist they come true instantly or you'll abandon them.

You have to be very fast in starting your journey but then be as slow as you need to be to infuse your business with stability. This book is about building an empire, and you cannot build anything strong without an equally strong foundation. You'll notice a consistent theme of subtracting desperation.

When businesses get desperate, they become average. A business with zero desperation, however, becomes a legacy. That's the way of life. I initially asserted that you look for opportunities that come your way in the form of help requests because then you're not the one chasing; you're being chased. Well, the opposite happens when you try to make money from your business too quickly because you don't have a job. As a result, you start chasing and lose credibility and prestige in the process. My method is, therefore, to keep my job helping rehabilitate people with disabilities and work on my magazine on my time off.

The Magic of Events

The digital age has come with great benefits but has simultaneously ushered in an era of laziness. Human beings are inclined towards laziness which is why they invent tools. But sometimes, effectiveness is lost in the process. Mass-manufactured products, for example, do not have the same charm as handmade items. Often we're willing to pay the price of this initial loss in return for a much greater price discount.

I am not here to judge whether this is the right or wrong choice when it comes to purchasing, but when it comes to spreading the word regarding your business, it is always wrong to sacrifice effectiveness for convenience. It is the most convenient to spam your link on a hundred different forums. It is definitely easier than picking up the phone. But guess what? Because it is easy, everyone's doing it. And when everyone's doing something, no one is doing it particularly well.

Events, I believe, are the hardest by comparison because you have to physically move and put yourself in a semi-exposed environment. It is much more comforting (and far less effective) to hide behind a screen. That's why there are fewer people at the events. The good news is that these people are more like-minded. They're personally invested in the ideas broadly relevant to the event because they made an effort to come there.

For your success, the first step is to find the right event. Selling artworks at a science fair is a bad idea. You can look up fairs, trade shows, and industry exhibits by spending a few minutes on Google.

The next thing is to look at where these events are taking place. Again, you must know your limits. If you cannot travel outside the state, there's no point in searching "networking events in the USA" instead;, you can simply search "networking events in Texas." Of course, you must replace Texas with whichever state or city you're in. With mobile phones, you can actually Google "networking events near me" and get proximity-filtered results.

Once you know which events you must go to, make sure you are prepared. Know what you'll say to introduce yourself. A short two-sentence intro, if prepared well, can make an impression that pays off for a lifetime. You should also avoid pitching your product or service right away. Instead, just network-to-network so you can expand your alliances and association to leverage at a later date. Remember, you must move fast and slow.

Going Digital

So far, I have spoken mostly about the analog and the offline world. I deliberately wanted to talk about that, as most people, I believe, skip the fundamentals and go straight to online. Yes, there are "digitally native" brands that started online and remained online, but every digital business has a real-world basis. If you get distracted and sold by the digital appearances, you'll build not a real business but an imitation of what you think a business is.

Masterclass is a digital education business, but the celebrity teachers on the platform have real-world credibility built offline. Similarly, when I took content from my magazine online, it was backed by a real-world interaction. I interviewed people for my print edition and took content from it, and put it online thanks to various apps that allow easy video making.

But I didn't go online just to go online. I was fueled by my desire to overexpose my work. Overexposure is the philosophy of making exposure the singular focus of your strategy. It is simply the result of the belief that "if a billion people know my work, I don't have to worry about my money." Attention is currency but to hold attention in a valuable manner is wealth. Currency comes and goes; it constantly flows. But wealth sticks around. And I wasn't in the business of getting attention by any means necessary. I wanted it on my own terms, and that's why I stuck to a few self-imposed limits.

For anyone looking to go online, you must have self-imposed boundaries that dictate how far you're willing to go to get exposure. I didn't cover gossip or scandals to get clicks. I didn't interview people while salivating for a large audience attached to their name. I interviewed solely with interest as my filter. If I liked the person I was talking to, I didn't care if not too many people would be attracted by their interview.

Ironically, that's what propelled my platform's growth. People started following out of interest because my interviews and conversations were authentic. We weren't chasing the greatest celebrities but people who had the most interesting life stories.

There's nothing more entertaining and interesting than a person's life, the greatest hits, distilled into twenty minutes. The interest this sparked wasn't engineered; it was just allowed to organically come about. When you're going digital, stay within the limits of your ethical boundaries, You might not attract everyone, but you'll attract enough people, and they'll be the right ones.

Bringing It All Together

Over the last few chapters, you've learned my secrets to business growth. We started with how paying attention to help requests helps one realize where opportunities lie. Then we moved onto how one can double down on these opportunities by specializing or scaling. But consistent throughout these pages was a theme of doing what you can with what you have. When I look at the success stories of different entrepreneurs, I see that they've leveraged the internet and the events space within their respective industries. That's what I aim to bring to my community.

I started to notice that the events I went to weren't well-managed. The organizers seemed more concerned with getting people in the door than the experience said people have upon attending. That's where I found my opportunity. Soon after, I hosted my first event, which was a roaring success despite being a small gathering. I didn't focus on spreading a wide net but on making sure everyone who attended found value.

Over the years, it has started growing, and the more people visit, the more opportunities everyone has. The idea is to bring local celebrities alongside people who often get ignored or overlooked because of lack of opportunity or visibility. When we bring such talented people to the forefront of their relevant market's attention, everyone wins.

Aside from events, I embraced the digital aspect of my business and have honed in on my social media presence as well as my website, where you can access various resources. So many people miss the point with print and try to shift their publications to "online only." The words aren't all that people buy when they subscribe to a magazine. It's about the feeling and the attention that is exclusive to paper. That's why I stand by my quarterly magazine alongside a monthly newsletter and an annual directory.

You'll notice that events, print publications, and online content are different avenues but have the same theme and mission: to help you connect with the opportunities and knowledge you need to succeed. And that's how you turn an individual business idea into an empire. People try to do too many things that are truly disconnected. That only produces a disjointed result at best or scatters one's focus at worst. You must always go back to the question of who you're helping, so everything you do produces a solo empire, not a scattered colony.

Brand Lessons

While being consistent across various domains with your mission helps, a mismatched brand can bring your empire crumbling. What's the solution? To have a brand that is reflective of your values. Let's briefly discuss my brand with this lesson in mind. I truly believe that we're all divine in one way or another because life, which reflects divinity, has touched us in one way or another and has shaped us through unique experiences. And since it all started with creating a resource that connects and continues to be a network of connections, I have decided to call it Divine Connections. The name has three properties: it is memorable, reflects a core reality of my business, and it holds true across all domains. Let's examine these in reverse.

The truth part is obvious in the fact that I do not do anything unless It is connecting people. The interviews I conduct tend to connect personalities to my readers. The events I hold tend to allow people to connect with one another, and the directory, of course, connects people to resources like businesses they can avail the services of. When you create a brand, you must make sure that the name reflects what's common and true across all your business propositions.

This brings us to the reality of the commonality. The fact that everything we do is connecting people in one way or another and that the word "connection" is also in our brand name makes the entire brand firmly grounded in reality. If your brand is not reflective of reality, it is pure fiction, and while fiction makes an impression, it doesn't outlast the real thing. Make a checklist for your businesses with two items: is it true to our brand values? Is it reflective of our reality?

Ultimately, your brand is not what you say it is. Your brand is what people come to expect of you. It wouldn't matter if I called my business "Divine Connections" if its result was alienating and disconnecting people. That's where we come to the final thing: being memorable. How's being memorable related to being honest and real? Well, if you're consistently real and honest, your audience will memorize what they must expect from you and build your brand for you.

Let It Flow

I don't want my explanation of the elements of my brand name to suggest that one should engineer theirs by trying to check the boxes. That would be, in essence, chasing that elusive name. Divine Connections as a name came to me when I was driving. It dropped into my consciousness. Since I knew that I wanted to uphold truthfulness and have a name that reflects reality, I knew I had stumbled onto the right thing. You must let your brand's name emerge spontaneously and adopt it when it checks all the boxes. In other words, let ideas flow and let go of ones that aren't memorable, reflective of reality, and truthful to your business's core identity.

Above all, remember that a brand isn't manufactured by you; it is organized by people. Whenever you try to force anything onto people, they will only rebel against it. Rebellion is in the human DNA. When businesses try to tell people what to think of them, people wholeheartedly reject the message. That's why the truly savvy businesses observe instead of creating. They realize wherever there is an opportunity to organize meaning and pounce at it when it rears its head.

For those of you who do not know, organizing meaning is a simple exercise in gently guiding people to find words and images that make sense of a set of truths they know. Think of a flag of a country. People come to build their opinions about a country through experience or spontaneous consumption of information. A flag then organizes it all into a package that they either hate or love.

In your business, the same is true with your reputation. You cannot "build" a reputation; you can only organize the different expectations people have of your business under a consistent visual or linguistic brand. People expect me to be helpful, people-oriented, and value-driven. It would be nice to push this idea without any effort, but I had to stay consistent with these values for over ten years. People, along the way, started to notice the consistency, which made it okay for me to organize it into a brand.

All in all, you don't even need to worry about the brand if you're honest and authentic. People follow your journey and start remembering that every time you launch a product or a service, it has certain characteristics. That leads me to the conclusion that your brand is the natural organization of things you cannot stop doing.

Where Does Your Confidence Come From?

I have noticed that some people seem to have a lot of confidence, but when one looks a little deeper, it turns out all that boisterousness is just loud insecurity. True confidence is content and calm, but more important than the demeanor of one's confidence is its source. Where does your confidence come from? Does it come from your looks? IF that's the case, you're in trouble because looks fade. Does it come from other people complimenting you? Because if that's the case, you're in trouble yet again because people can flip like a coin toss. Your confidence must be internally generated, so you don't rely on others for self-worth.

You must shut out the sources of confidence that are time-bound and not perpetually present. People's words, Arbitrary titles, who you date, how you look, and what your status is within a particular community are all unreliable sources of confidence. Why is that? Simply because none of these things last. Life has its ups and downs, and you cannot let your confidence go along for the ride. Regardless of whether you're at the top of the world or getting your serving of life's lemons, you must have high levels of confidence.

That's only possible if it is internally generated. "But, Deloris, I don't think I am that confident," at least 50% of my readers will think. I had the great privilege of having a family that instilled internal confidence in me, but I also had the pleasure of meeting great businesswomen who had to overcome self-doubt. I also was taught to trust God, have faith, and I can do all things through Christ. Here's a nugget of wisdom I would like to share from their experiences:

You can build your self-confidence through competence. Look at one thing you are good at. This can be anything. You might have the urge to diminish or dismiss it as tiny. Or insignificant. Do not give in to this urge. Instead, double down on how great you are at this one thing. Repeat it out loud if you have to. For reference, I will present something that you might dismiss but is totally valid for this exercise. "I can cook the perfect lasagna," you can say over and over till you start feeling a little confident.

You'll notice your posture change. As you repeat this, start thinking about victories in your life. The smallest wins. And as they come to mind, start adding them to your chants. "I make the perfect lasagna, got the best grades in school twenty years ago, and can iron my clothes in under a minute." On the surface, this might sound silly, but on a deeper level, you're shifting your consciousness to see what you do right instead of beating yourself over what you do wrong.

Your "Aha" Motivation

Confidence is only one part of the success equation. The second part is perhaps harder to maintain: it is your motivation. When you're trying to stay motivated, failure isn't as big a danger as getting good enough. When Divine Connections got enough advertisers for me to be able to buy a few nice things while keeping my day job, it became really lucrative to just keep the business on that level. Why go the extra mile? Things are good enough, aren't they? That's why you have to look for the "Aha!" motivation.

With your "Aha!" motivation, you're not driven by the logical desires of ease and comfort. Remember, ease and comfort don't go hand in hand with greatness, and the last thing you want is to give up your momentum and settle for "good enough" only to kick yourself later for not pursuing excellence. With that established, let me explain what "Aha!" motivation is and why it is called that.

When I was a kid, my dad used to tell me if I was smart with my money and saved up, I would one day be able to buy my own house. Guess what I did when I saved up money as an adult? I bought my place. I did not tell my parents. One day I told them that we were going to our cousins and ask them to follow me. This was a perfect surprise. I brought them to my house and then informed them that it was mine. That was the "Aha!" moment I was sacrificing so much for.

I could have gotten a nice place to rent with a little bit of money. That would be comfy but wouldn't create that "Aha!" moment. Whether your moment is to show an ex that they wronged the wrong person or show people who underestimated you that they were wrong, it is a powerful tool to motivate you when logic points towards mediocrity. Remember, the majority of the people aren't willing to shoot for the moon because, logically, life's good enough being average.

But if you're reading this book, I am sure you're not content with "average" or "good enough." At this point, most people will know exactly what their "Aha!" moment is going to be. But some might not have any such moment. To them, I would say, simply make a list of people who believed in you or ones who didn't. Proving the first right and the second wrong is how you create your "Aha!" motivation.

Check Your Finances

It doesn't matter how motivated you are to do the right thing if you don't know what the right thing is. You could be highly motivated to go from Texas to California, but if you keep driving in the wrong direction, you'll not have the right results. You could technically keep going and circle around the globe to eventually reach Cali, but we know the best way to go about it is to point in the right direction, to begin with. And since every material transaction in this world directly or indirectly links to money, we have to get one thing right: finances.

If you get your money right, a lot of things in your life will automatically fall into place. But if this aspect is wrong, you'll not only have issues in other areas, but you'll not even realize that you have true trouble with your money. Wealth, especially monetary wealth, is such a touchy subject that we don't even talk about it with others. I find it quite sad that we don't even acknowledge it personally.

When I was saving up money, I lived with my cousins, and we split bills. Too many people sacrifice their finances to their pride. The problem with sacrificing money for pride is that you eventually end up needing money so much that you lose your pride in the process.

I am able to build my business gradually because I'm not wasting so much money that I need too much from my business. Not only does this keep my business free of pressure, but it also incentivizes me to think of the value I am giving my audience.

When you do not care about your finances or don't pay attention to them, money flows away from you. Remember, human beings' ability to spend is infinite, while no business's ability to generate wealth is infinite. And there lies the problem with most entrepreneurs' journey. If you start a business without building your discipline to hold cash, you end up spending what you make instead of reinvesting it in your business. And when you don't reinvest in your business, you let your competition get ahead. How, though?

Because no matter the market you're in, there's a Deloris there. And if you don't become the Deloris in your space, someone else will. While you buy your sneakers or spend money on a night out, someone is living with her cousins and spending money marketing her business, buying ads in Divine Connections Magazine, and investing in events to make more money and steal your customers.

When Entrepreneurship Is Alien

In the previous chapter, we dove deeper in the direction of finance. But it isn't obvious that that's the only direction one needs to be a successful business owner. We need to have specific tactics, mindset, and business knowledge that's missing for the broadest section of our population. While I had the privilege of belonging to a family that motivated me and believed in me, I did not have access to entrepreneurship knowledge within my household.

Thankfully I was interested enough in the world of business to get over this and connect with entrepreneurs myself. Had I been naturally too reserved, I might have missed out on valuable lessons. Without these lessons, I would be learning from my own mistakes and losing my motivation, and more importantly, my time in the process.

Fortunately, I was blessed with the confidence to connect. Now, I think about others and wonder the same. What if today, there's a Deloris out there who has much more value to offer the world than I do, but she's held back by the fact that entrepreneurship is foreign to her as well. Except, she doesn't have the connections I made. This thought used to disturb me a lot. That's why I have focused on building a unique atmosphere in my business events where visitors can connect with each other without feeling awkward.

There's an air of intimacy and belonging at events organized by Divine Connections. Everyone's expecting to talk and be talked to. You don't face the dread of potential rejection, and I invite genuinely warm and accomplished personalities to give valuable lessons from the stage. That's the beauty of a social person getting ahead and wanting to bring others along. I don't feel like I need to get ahead for my sake as much as I want to grow with a community of people I love.

If you want to be a business owner, you must understand that cutting short your learning curve is the single most valuable thing you can do for yourself. And to do so in an effective manner, you need to learn from other entrepreneurs. It is entirely valid to get this information from your friends and family if they own even a single business among all of them. But if no one you know is a successful business owner, you have to connect with those who are. For that, you've got to check out our events!

The Power of Subtracting Demotivation

The motivational speaking industry is a multi-million dollar machine because it isn't based on a one-off transaction. When you listen to a business owner, you don't become permanently motivated. And I believe the reason we need repeated injections of motivation is that we are surrounded by demotivating people. From news channels to online content commentary, everything is oriented towards negativity. As a result, people lose their motivation bit by bit until they need a life-saving jab from a world-class motivational speaker.

These speakers do a lot of good, but I believe they treat the symptoms, not the underlying cause. There's a saying that fish don't know that water is wet. Similarly, you don't know which ever-present elements in your life are harmful. If you've grown up with haters around, you'll not know the incredible benefit of having an environment without a single demotivational individual.

Well, that's the environment I grew up in. Not one member of my family was negative. No one was pessimistic about my potential, and this helped me avoid making friends who are continuously negative. Many people grow up with negativity in their homes, and since they see such attitudes as normal, they do not draw the line when making friends. Having negative friends is like having a paper shredder as your wallet. You'll lose all your money with such a wallet. Well, you lose all your energy and motivation with such friends. And losing energy is no different than losing money.

I don't think I need to make a stronger case for subtracting demotivation from your surroundings. It is as obvious a dictum as "don't burn your money." The reason people don't subtract demotivation from their environment is simply that they don't know how to go about it. And I believe the best way to do so is to replace and fade.

When you try to "cut off" negative friends, you might be tempted to make a show of it. But such confrontations will only exhaust you and give your friends the opportunity to emotionally blackmail you into "Staying." Instead, it is much more straightforward to simply make better friends and gradually fade out your previous friendships. No one is hurt in the process, and you realize that the friend you stopped hanging out with, don't miss you either. But if you try to make a show of walking out, they'll fight to keep you around even though they wouldn't have missed your presence.

Refuse to Waste Time

This chapter requires your complete attention because we're talking about a very nuanced subject. When I started my magazine, I had no formal education in business or marketing. What I had was willpower and unwillingness to depend on others for help. And this saved me a lot of time. I have come to realize since that depending on others is a waste of time. But this knowledge served me to a degree. As my workload expanded and I needed to get more done, my insistence on clinging to old notions was getting in my way.

I now have an editor to help me out. It turns out that while depending on others to fix things for you is a major waste of time, so is refusing help when you need it. Ultimately you should value your time and let circumstances assist you in determining whether others are welcome in your mission or you need to cut weight and go solo.

Earlier, had I sought help while doing nothing for myself, I would have wasted significant time. But now, I would be wasting my time doing minor tasks when major tasks need my attention. And that's why depending on others is not just the right thing but the necessary thing. This is where trust and reliability come into play, but I'll leave those topics for a different chapter since they are complicated.

For now, you must internalize the message that you must value your time as much as celebrities and billionaires value theirs. You value your time for your time to become valuable. If a government prints a lot of money, guess what happens to the currency? It gets devalued. If you oversupply your time, you end up devaluing it. Make sure you hold your time and attention in high regard. Don't waste it on ads, mindless spending, and unproductive endeavors.

That said, we need to look at time wasters that are carefully disguised as productive activities. These are especially sinister since they avoid detection while harming your overall odds of success.

- Over-analyzing: This is the chief time-waster and gets discounted as research. You need action more than research, and any research that comes at the cost of action is not worth it.
- Distracted work: Yes, working is a waste of time if you do it in an unfocused manner. Your brain loses energy by switching between different modes. Do your work in large blocks of time so you can be more effective.

Integrity and Its Lack Are Contagious

While time-wasting is a plague that destroys businesses left and right, the bigger problem lies in the lack of integrity that is so seductive to new entrepreneurs. There's a reason why "get rich quick" schemes outsell slow and patient business building guides. Unfortunately, not many people want to get rich slowly, and the most surefire to get rich actually is to do so slowly. I don't mind the pace at which people advance. I think comparing yourself to others is the reason you might be tempted to cut corners.

Everyone has their own pace. You might have more privilege than me or fewer resources than me. That's why it is unfair that I judge myself by comparing my progress to yours. We may be the same age, but we didn't live the same life. I didn't have to worry about transportation; my parents got me a car. I didn't have to pay for school. I didn't have negativity around me. But at the same time, there are those my age who started out with a lot more money. Of course, they'll be ahead of me financially. How's that even a question. Where others my age are doesn't say anything about me, but what I do to catch up with them says volumes.

I noticed that some business owners in my circle boldly lacked integrity. Not only did they compromise their alleged values for a quick buck, but they seemed to show no remorse. In fact, they were proud of it and seemed to think that not being bound by morality was their superpower. I had to disassociate and distance myself from them because I did not want to teach my subconscious to treat lack of integrity as normal.

What many people don't realize is the fact that values and attitudes are contagious. Humans are social beings with thousands of years of honing social sensitivity. We pick up things from our surroundings, and if anything is common among most people around us, we normalize and adopt it. That's why accents exist and rub off across time.

Please don't let lack of integrity rub off on you. You might need to say farewell to friends and even partners in the process, but any time you pick your values and integrity over a connection with someone who lacks integrity, you make the right decision. Hang out with those who have integrity because it, too, as its absence, is contagious.

Trust Is A Resource

If I have had any struggle in my journey, it is this. While my business and industry revolve around connecting, it was hard for me to trust people. And that's like being really short and wanting to compete in the NBA. There are certain things we take for granted until we enter a specific niche where those things are valuable assets. Trust, and the ability to trust are both valuable resources.

There are many reasons to trust people and just as many not to trust them. And my solution is to hone my people-reading skills. If you can tell whether someone is a good person or unreliable, you'll be able to trust the right people. Ultimately it isn't trust or its lack that hurts, but trusting or distrusting the wrong person that causes a lot of pain and significant regrets. Let me give you an example.

If you trust a scammer, it is quite obvious how you would be hurt. But we rarely look at alternative scenarios where refusing to trust can be an obstacle. Here's one: if Peter Theil decided to mistrust Mark Zuckerberg when he asked for an investment, he wouldn't have turned his hundred thousand dollars into a million dollars.

Sometimes it isn't trust, but its lack that ends up costing you money. So, let's explore different ways in which we can expand our ability to give and get trust. It is a two-way street, and since you need people to trust, you must not come off as stand-offish.

Start with low risk

Begin your journey towards cultivating your ability to trust by trusting people within a low-stakes context. It is easier to trust someone with $15 than $150. This will allow you to gradually expand your comfort zone when it comes to trusting people.

Get better at reading people.

Don't judge people by their appearances but by their actions. Actions don't need to be visible gestures. Look at their hidden ones. Look at how they treat others, what they say about people behind their backs, and what seems to motivate them. Each of these is a valuable tool that gives you insights into whether you can trust someone or not.

Create degrees of trust

Most of us are so black and white with our trust, and this is what makes trust so risky. If trusting someone means blindly following them, of course, you're going to be apprehensive. Learn to trust a little and then gradually trust more as the person shows he or she deserves more.

People Are As Good As Their Word

Continuing the theme of trust, we have to talk about the number one way people reveal their unreliability: by not keeping their word. I used to get so frustrated when I would invite someone to my event and create my entire marketing campaign and schedule around their presence, only for them to tell me last minute that they can't make it because of "some stuff" that allegedly came up. It used to drive me up the wall, but now I get excited. Why?

Because it is better that I learn about someone's lack of trustworthiness, reliability, and integrity before getting too deep in business with them. Of course, this doesn't mean one has to get burned every time just to learn the same lesson. I've gotten increasingly selective about who I do business with primarily because I can now pick up on who is going to show up and who won't.

Logic has helped me through this as I realized that people who have more to gain from attending would do so out of self-interest. This has allowed me to make my events more valuable for all parties. I cannot sit around waiting for people to become more reliable. I believe that's a waste of time. Instead, I've started paying attention to people's words. And I suggest you do too.

But there's no point in looking at others without considering yourself. Remember that it isn't just people's words that reflect their character. What you say matters. On the obvious level, one can see that sticking to one's word is a great practice. But there's something deeper to consider too. The positivity (or the lack of it) in your word reflects your mindset.

When you say you'll "be there," you're saying something completely different from when you say "you'll make it there." These nuances show your enthusiasm and self-belief. Using words that reflect certainty does not help you earn others' trust. Would you board a plane if the pilot said, "we might be safe." No, you need the person you trust to show he or she is worthy of the trust by being as confident as possible.

Confidence and arrogance aren't the same things. That's why I advise using confident language but avoid unnecessary hyperbole. Hyperbolic exaggeration debases the value and trustworthiness of your words. And as a magazine business owner, I know for a fact that words are powerful.

Never Subtract Your Identity

My relationship with God is pretty dear to me, and I will not leave it out of this book. I know this might make some people unhappy, but I do not believe in sacrificing authenticity and honesty to make everyone happy. That is always a bad choice because one cannot make everyone happy no matter what one does. Never subtract your identity from your business because it is seeing a part of yourself in your business that keeps you sufficiently attached to it. I don't have children, but I see my business as my baby.

And while some business owners might cheat and cut corners to get ahead, I will not compromise or devalue my business that way. Why? Because it is an extension of my identity. I received inspiration for the word from God. I also have gospel groups show up at my events, and the word "divine" is in my business name. Even though it might be tough for some to believe, I didn't write this chapter to preach about God even though I believe faith helps one get over obstacles.

I wrote this chapter to emphasize that you must stay true to your identity in your business. You might not even believe in God. and if you don't, all I say is don't pretend you do. A business that doesn't possess the characteristics of its owner is just an attempt to make a quick buck, and we all know how that turns out.

Now let's address the question of how you should know which values to add to your business, so it accurately seeds your identity into its foundations. I would simply say to keep doing what you feel like doing. Your identity incorporates your tastes and preferences, which means you'll want to add things that represent you. It is only when you start consciously censoring your desires for others' sake that you falsify your business identity.

I truly want to include God in my business, and that does turn off some people. The best I can do is refuse to judge them. If they judge me, that's not my problem. If I judge myself and censor myself to appease them, then that's my problem, and that's a big problem. All in all, when you go about building your business, please avoid changing what you want to do just, so it makes everyone comfortable. Stand by your identity.

Age Is An Asset

Are you ready to discover a mistake that most entrepreneurs make when they get a little bit of success? Not considering age groups. Suppose you get some amount of money flowing in after you put your product out there. What do you do next? If you're like most business owners, you'll continue to do what's working without looking into what is actually working.

Yes, that's something that differentiates regular business owners from excellent ones. Generally, people see things that work and the things that don't work. What a select few, and you now, know is that among the things that are working, some things are working more than other things. Bringing this abstract concept to a tactical reality, I'll bring up the example of age groups. Why do you think Facebook and other platforms that allow advertisers to serve marketing messages insist on collecting age data? Because people of different age groups have different interests. If you're smart, the first thing you would do upon noticing the success of your products is single out the age group that makes up the majority of your customers. The next step is to double down on that age group by focusing on them with your marketing. Start tweaking your product to fit them more precisely.

That's no secret, though. Most businesses do this, albeit unintentionally. A Youth Streetwear brand rarely has elements that appeal to older people. Similarly, McDonald's kids' meals don't have portions or marketing to appeal to even teenagers. The secret weapon of a new entrepreneur is to roll out different products for different age groups. McDonald's does not sell kids' meals exclusively. Think about that. This is one of the largest fast-food businesses in the world, and it refuses to commit to a single age group. Why? Because it is too big.

Now, if you want to have a small business that stays small and is constantly plagued by insecurity and sudden shifts in the economy, by all means, serve only a small market. But I want my business to take over the world, and that's why I have to create different categories. As I write this, I am planning on a kids' event where younger people can get connected to opportunities and knowledge. I have also dabbled into doing events for seniors. McDonald's doesn't refuse to only target one age group because it is too big. It got too big because it continued to serve everyone.

Change Things Up

Businesses cannot afford to be boring. Boredom is death to a business because sales require attention, and attention can never be forced; it must be solicited with intrigue and fascination. Let's explore different ways to change things up in a meaningful way because shaking things up just to shake things up is a formula for diluting your brand. You must be intentional about each change, so you don't build a reputation for doing things without purpose or meaning.

One of the best changes I made was through themes. I picked "mother" as the theme for mother's day. Soliciting memories, experiences, and stories from the people I interviewed, I created a nice montage of content that paid tribute to the mothers around us. Even people who feel like mothers because of various reasons loved the content. I remember talking to a 67-year-old man who told me there was no way he could fit the highlights of his memories with his mother in a single paragraph. Such stories remind me of why I started my business in the first place.

Think about how you can change up things in your business. Usually, you will have opportunities related to your product and business category and opportunities related to general themes. Themes don't just need to be "special days" in the year. While doing something for Valentine's day might be right for a restaurant, I doubt that that's relevant to a car mechanic's business. And if a car mechanic tried to do some kind of a deal for that day, it would seem shoehorned and inauthentic.

Fashion brands eventually started creating face masks when wearing one became the norm. That is an example of how themes that are relevant to a product don't need to be international days of celebration. The best way to keep up with such themes is to have an Ideapad.

An Ideapad or an idea notepad is literally a notepad you keep on your person, so whenever you have an idea, you can note it and keep it from disappearing through distractions. More importantly, you anticipate ideas by keeping a notepad. Trust me, I wish I could write down different ways you could change things up, but by virtue of putting them to paper, I would have destroyed their uniqueness. Your ideas will drop into your consciousness once you start expecting them. Just make sure you're not shoehorning your business into a theme that it doesn't belong to.

Pay Attention To Feedback

"I don't care what people think" is a cool phrase that shows one's self-assurance but angers me. It angers me not because it offends me. I get worked up about it because it is a lie. And people who pretend they aren't affected by others' opinions usually are the most impacted by them. Humans are social beings, and caring about the general feedback is usually a good thing. Of course, if you're surrounded by toxic people, you need to harden your walls and not take their words seriously, but you have to pay attention to feedback.

If you're in business, somebody has to care about your product. If no one cares, then you're your only customer. Not only do your customers need to care, but your amplifiers need to care as well. "What are my amplifiers?" you may ask. Amplifiers are people who can elevate your exposure and bring your business to a new level. I've been nominated for many awards but haven't really visited any award shows. The Gospel Choice Awards nomination got me quite excited.

Award shows can be great platforms to promote your business. I include awards in my events for the same reason. I truly believe they can amplify people's personal messages and elevate their brands. But for me, award nominations serve as feedback. It shows me who is watching. And while these kinds of feedback indicate excellence, there's one type of feedback that is superior to everything else: repeat transaction.

The prestige of awards, the value of coverage, and the kind words of your friends cannot all trump the value of a customer purchasing your product or service and coming back for more. That's the complement of the highest order and the feedback you should truly gear your business for.

The alternative is true as well. I don't care if you make a million dollars doing business with people who do not buy anything from you again. That's not a victory because there are a million ways to lose a million dollars in a few years. And if people aren't coming back to your business for more, you're not going to be in business for long. From Amazon to Walmart, every big business makes its money from subscriptions. Even more exclusive brands like Ferrari have a high referral rate and, believe it or not, an average transaction frequency of 1+ across a lifetime.

Take One Unit of Time
At A Time

So many people I know make the mistake of trying to do too much in a short amount of time. This is not only detrimental to their long-term business success but also counters the wisdom of the ages. Time moves slow, and it is only the false sense of urgency that makes people believe it is moving fast. Take one unit of time at a time and do your best in it. Remember, the future will not sneak up on you. There's no way your life ten years from now will happen tomorrow, but what you do today will most definitely impact your life ten years from now.

It is a hard concept to grasp and internalize because we perceive time in such a slow manner yet recall memories on a large scale. I have taken one year of execution at one time. That way, while I can have a vision for the future, I can concern myself with doing the best I can with what I have in the short term. I throw an event at the end of the year to acknowledge that I have had a year well-spent. By well-spent, I don't mean a year of luxury. I mean a year of making connections, serving my marketing, and most importantly, learning.

Having your goals is really important. You must have your daily goals as well as your weekly, monthly, and annual goals. Daily goals aren't things you pick out every day, as that would be a waste of time. Imagine spending an hour every day to think what you'll try to accomplish that day. That will accomplish one thing for sure: a waste of 365 days in a year.

Daily goals are more like set-and-forget type chains. Create a chain that you do not want to break. This was done most famously by Seinfeld, who wrote a joke a day. And every day that he wrote a joke, he put an X on his calendar. After a few days, he did not want to break the chain, so he continued meeting his daily target.

Weekly goals can be thought up once a month alongside your monthly targets. As long as you take care of these, your annual goals should automatically be fulfilled. If you eat right and exercise every day, you cannot help but end up obese at the end of the year.

How to Navigate Crisis

If you have a business, you'll have crises, and if you're going to keep your business, you'll need to get good at crisis management. Fortunately for you, I have a few lessons that were learned through up close experience with multiple crises. These lessons are explored in the rest of this chapter. While this will serve as a good foundation, nothing beats drawing from a broad range of sources. You can get in touch with The Divine Connections ticket sales team for more information on how you can learn from a variety of entrepreneurs.

Speaking of ticket sales, one of the most recent crises that are quite fresh in my memory is the COVID-19 pandemic. I had sold tickets for my event and booked the speakers, but the state rules made it impossible to have even a small-scale gathering. My initial plan was to simply do smaller-scale events that ensure everyone gets to be a part of a version of what's usually our big event. Think of it as a movie screening as opposed to a theatre opening. At a Broadway show, everyone watches the play together. At a movie screening, the same movie is seen by different people at different times.

I thought I had it covered when the people concerned got back to me with their answer: no small gatherings either. That's when I had to postpone the event, and that's also the most important lesson. Crisis management is simply the art of doing the best you can with what you have.

Because I had no legal way of moving forward, I simply postponed it. And in the meantime, I had one thing: time. I used it to keep my audience interested while learning to navigate the digital events space. By the time we could move forward with our event, I was able to not only have a physical event but allow digital participation as well. This actually increased the revenue for the event compared to what it would have been had the event not happened.

That's my second and final point: when a crisis hits, heighten your standards. Don't just try to fix the problem but try to turn the situation to your advantage. Ask yourself, "what can I do so that things are better because of this obstacle than they would have been had it not happened." That question alone will guide you to go beyond survival mode and get really creative with your crisis management. All the best.

Create Systems of Appreciation

I wanted to recognize and honor people I admired, so I started dabbling into awards. Within our first year, we had 300 nominees, and from that, I discovered how rewarding it is to reward others for their genuine value. I have since learned more about how to best distribute appreciation and gratitude. Even if you don't want to run your own awards show someday, I urge you to read on and learn about systemizing appreciation. This will help you have a better social life, and your love life too will blossom because gratitude makes the world go around.

Why do we need to appreciate those around us daily? That's the first question. We're all grateful at certain moments across a month or two. The point of creating systems of gratitude is to make the act of being grateful a regular thing. And the reason you must be grateful regularly is that it orients you towards noticing your blessing. Your life isn't the things you own; it is what you experience. There's no point or value to having blessings around you if you aren't even noticing them, much less appreciating them. A system of gratitude will allow you to appreciate your blessings.

An award show is a system of distributing appreciation on an annual basis. How does that translate to one's personal life? Well, let's deconstruct the process of an award show so we can apply it on a smaller scale and edit it to fit a personal setting. An award show's producer constantly asks two questions: What categories should we have? Who fits in those categories? On a personal level, you must ask, "what should I appreciate?" and "whom should I appreciate for those 'whats'?" For example, I might have a "breakthrough entrepreneur of the year" category. Here, I appreciate the emergence of new value in the business world. And for that, the producer looks for people who've contributed by breaking onto the scene.

When you ask a similar question, you get a more personal answer. "What should I be appreciative of?" and you'll probably conclude you should be grateful for the helping hand you get around the house. The next question is the "whom" question, and for it, you might have your husband, child, or sibling as the nominee. The winner gets a genuine compliment. Treat your "I'm grateful" as a trophy and make sure you give two trophies a day. It will change your life.

Motivations Must Shift to Keep The Journey Going

In the previous chapter, we discussed how being motivated to find recipients for gratitude will make you count your blessings. Here we talk about motivations in general with business success in mind. As I write this book, I have enough money to carry me for months to come. In other words, I can pause or stop my side business if I want to. These moments are great for reflection because I get to ask myself, "was I in this for the money?" and "Do I want to continue doing this?" Remember, your younger self is committed to a path, and you're not beholden to the things you thought you wanted when you were younger.

Continuing or diverting your path are both valid, and you shouldn't feel ashamed either way. What matters is that you seek your happiness and don't hurt people in the process. That said, you must know that your motivations will shift. You'll start off with the motivation to minimize the struggle. We all do. Humans love to minimize struggle, and that's why we have mass agriculture and cars. But once you're past the point of "seeking comfort," you need to have a different set of motivations. And here's the tricky part: you need to set these motivations pre-struggle.

If you're struggling and your main motivation is "to get enough money to cover the rent and have something leftover," you'll no longer have the motivation to carry on once you reach that goal. You cannot talk yourself into a different goal. But if you set a goal to "have enough money left over to feed a hundred families," you'll keep going past comfort and continue earning more and making more of an impact in the process. That, however, is easier said than done. Because when you're setting a selfless goal, your personal preservation instinct is shouting, "Hey, why the 100 families? You barely live paycheck to paycheck yourself!"

And that's why you must use the anticipated motivation method. In other words, you'll acknowledge that initially, you're interested in putting an end to your struggle. You'll tell yourself that your first milestone is to get out of the paycheck-to-paycheck environment. And once you're out of that position, you promise yourself; you'll keep going to help feed 100 other families (or whatever your 'past comfort' goal is). Ultimately, it is all about anticipating the fact that you'll reach a level of comfort and deciding beforehand what will keep you going when you reach there.

Are You Your Worst Enemy?

If you look back at the chapters in this book, you'll notice that there's a consistent theme of nuance and its need in almost every dimension. For example, with motivation, I acknowledged that if you're too selfless, you'll not believe your own mission and abandon it in order to get yourself out of a bad position. Similarly, with not relying on others, I mentioned how it could be a waste of time to wait for others to fix things but can also be a waste of your time to insist you do the minor things that others can help you with. Nuance, I believe, is much needed, and it is needed the most when it comes to personal responsibility.

When you give up personal responsibility, you become the perpetual victim who continues to blame others for everything. Such people are hard to respect and even harder to help. Ultimately no one can help someone who isn't willing to help himself or herself. And that's why one must take self-responsibility. The issue with taking it to an extreme is that it turns into self-blame. And this is something I kind of gravitated towards in the earlier years of my entrepreneur journey. That made my worst enemy.

It did more good than bad, I must say. Had I been inclined to the other extreme, I would have totally lost any ability to do things for myself. But this extreme wasn't great either. Sure, I took responsibility for things in my control, but I also ended up blaming myself for factors outside my control. If I had the same level of "being my own enemy" this year (2021, as of the writing of this book) as I used to back in the day, I would have doubted myself because of the COVID-19 crisis. You can see how problematic that is, right?

While COVID-19 devastated businesses across the globe, there are many business owners who are doubting themselves for starting their business or taking a chance on their dreams. This is horrible because it isn't their fault that such a pandemic changed everything. We could not have seen this coming, and it is time we stop pretending. Give yourself credit and only take responsibility for what's in your control. Acknowledge when it is someone else's fault or no one's fault so you can give yourself a break because otherwise, no matter how high-functioning you are, you will end up being your own worst enemy.

The Final Leap

Since this is the final chapter, it is high time we talk about the final leap. What is the final leap? It is the stage where you transition from being a part-time business owner to a full-time business owner. It is when you graduate your side-hustle and christen it with the title of "business." In his chapter, we will go over the prerequisites, and when you know, you've reached that point. As you know, I am not a big fan of starting a business out of nowhere with nothing else to do except building your business. There's too much uncertainty in such a style of business, and it forces business owners to focus on short-term gains.

That's why I support the idea of having a job and starting a side-hustle. IT is what I have done, and it has filled my life with stability and has simultaneously fulfilled me. It is also why I have had enough gas to run my business authentically without compromise for over ten years. When does one switch to full-time business ownership? And I believe the first thing one has to ask is, "why should I switch?" If your motivation is simply that you've always wanted to be a full-time entrepreneur, you're going in with the wrong motivation.

You should switch to full-time business management as a duty, not a hobby. As a hobby, your business should always be a side hustle. Only when it needs your attention full-time is there an actual room for you to shift. Still, it might be unwise to take that final leap because the fact that your business needs full-time attention doesn't mean it is worth that full-time attention.

If you want to start a farm and you work a job away from farmland or rural areas, you cannot do this as a side hustle. And while your farm will need your full-time attention, if it can't cover your bills, it isn't worth your full-time attention. You might have to pay workers to work full-time, but you have to keep your job. Whatever pays you the highest should have your service until your business becomes valuable enough that you're actually losing money by holding your job.

And circling back to the theme of honesty, I will be honest I am not there yet. My business has created connections worth over $10 million, but its revenue isn't at the point where it is worth it for me to leave my job and focus on it. But I am entering the phase where I will make my final leap. And the lesson for you right now is that it is okay if you don't make your transition for the next decade. What matters is that you do what you're meant to do daily and enjoy yourself.

Excellence or Nothing at All

I'll leave you with a motto that simultaneously motivates you and serves as practical advice: don't go halfway. Prepare for the long run and pick the thing that you can pursue excellence in. Give it your best shot, or avoid it altogether. Excellence or nothing at all has been my mode of operation since the inception of Divine Connections. Back when it was only a directory of resources, I tried my best to make it an excellent resource. I didn't venture into events till I could make them excellent. Make excellence your brand by refusing to do anything else. Make great things and never lower your standards. Thank you for reading my book, and I hope you join Divine Connections as we continue to make good things excellent.

About The Author

Publisher. Game-Changer. CEO. Master Networker for Marketplace Ministry. Kingdom Advocate.

These are a few of the many titles that speak of the visionary, connector, and powerhouse, Deloris Williams. A native of Durham, NC, and resident of the High Point-Greensboro, NC area, Williams exhibited a keen sense of finance, money management and entrepreneurship at an early age. Upon graduating from Winston Salem State University with no college debt, Williams also became a titleholder of a note-free vehicle and a custom-built home built, all before the age of 27. Williams went on to conceptualize a faith-based quarterly magazine publication aimed to connect Christian and religious organizations across the country. This publication features gospel artists, authors, pastors, and entrepreneurs, and through the magazine's impactful features, readers become inspired to discover their fullest potential in lifestyle, spirit, and business. The magazine also serves as an essential networking tool for marketplace ministry business owners to maximize the kingdom impact.

Williams is also the Founder and CEO of Divine Connections; a business stemmed in assisting faith-based and other prominent and aspiring businesses to connect and unlock their greatness. By way of the magazine publication, newsletters, and internet TV channel, Divine Connections, hosts impactful community networking events, geared to engage divine connections and critical relationships for leverage in society and the kingdom of God. Her passion and gift are to spread and uplift the community and touch the nation through positivity.

Williams is a recipient of The Gospel Choice Awards for Magazine of the Year and Media Ministry of the Year. She was also prestigiously nominated for Magazine of the Year from S & M Indie Awards. Her publication, Divine Connections Magazine, has been recognized as the top magazine for S & M Radio. Also, she received a nomination for The Gospel Image (Best Gospel Magazine Award) and Dunamis Award for Media Publication of the year.

In 2013, Williams became an author of the critically acclaimed book; You *Can Do It: Make it Happen & Handle your Business*, a stirring volume in which Williams shares her tried and true keys to empowerment and dream execution. Currently she is the author of her second book, "How to build and empire helping People. " Along with her roles as author, award-winning publisher, and entrepreneur, Williams is a skilled actress, being most recently featured in a significant character role in the hit play, "Sinderella."

Ultimately, Williams' accomplishments serve as a living testament of her heart for God and people and exhibit the power of sharing her gifts and journey with others. Throughout her life, she serves as an example to all with whom she comes in contact, proving that we all can accomplish the "impossible."

Connect With Me

Stay connected with Deloris Williams for more information, advertise, be a sponsor, or support

Email @ divineconnectionsmagazine@gmail.com
TEXT 336.338.8903
Facebook: www.facebook.com/divineconnectionsmarketing
Instagram: **divineconnections**
LinkedIn: www.linkedin.com/in/deloriswilliams-divineconnections
YouTube:www.youtube.com/thedivineconnections

For More information go to
https://linktr.ee/DelorisWilliams

P.O. BOX 16259
High Point, NC 27261